MW01681646
THIS *journal* BELONGS TO:

Freebies

www.papeteriebleu.com/dotjournal

DOWNLOAD CODE: JRNL264

74628853R00061

Made in the USA
Lexington, KY
15 December 2017